The Prodigal Son

Illustrated Lyrics of Faith

Based on the song by Joe Guadagno

Hear the song on Spotify!   Hear the song on Apple Music!   Hear the song on YouTube!

by Joe Guadagno

and Victoria Winifred

The Prodigal Son:
Illustrated Lyrics of Faith
©2024 Joe Guadagno and Victoria Winifred.

Published by The Enrichment Connection.
Paperback ISBN: 979-8-9869675-9-2
1st Edition

All Rights Reserved. No part of this book may be reproduced or transmitted in any form or by any means whatsoever without express written permission from the author, except in the case of brief quotations embodied in critical articles and reviews. Please refer all pertinent questions to The Enrichment Connection at enrichmentconnection@gmail.com.

DISCLAIMER: This work is based on a biblical parable and includes lyrics from the song "The Prodigal Son," written and recorded by the author, Joe Guadagno. While the characters, places, events, and incidents may be inspired by the parable, they have been adapted and reinterpreted by the author. Any resemblance to actual persons, living or dead, outside of the biblical context, is purely coincidental. This work also includes passages from the Bible. Unless otherwise indicated, all Scripture quotations are from the King James Version (KJV), which is in the public domain.

All of Joe Guadagno's music is available on most major music streaming platforms, either under his name or his band's name, JGnFriends.

With gratitude to the Lord,
who always welcomes
the wanderer home
with open arms.

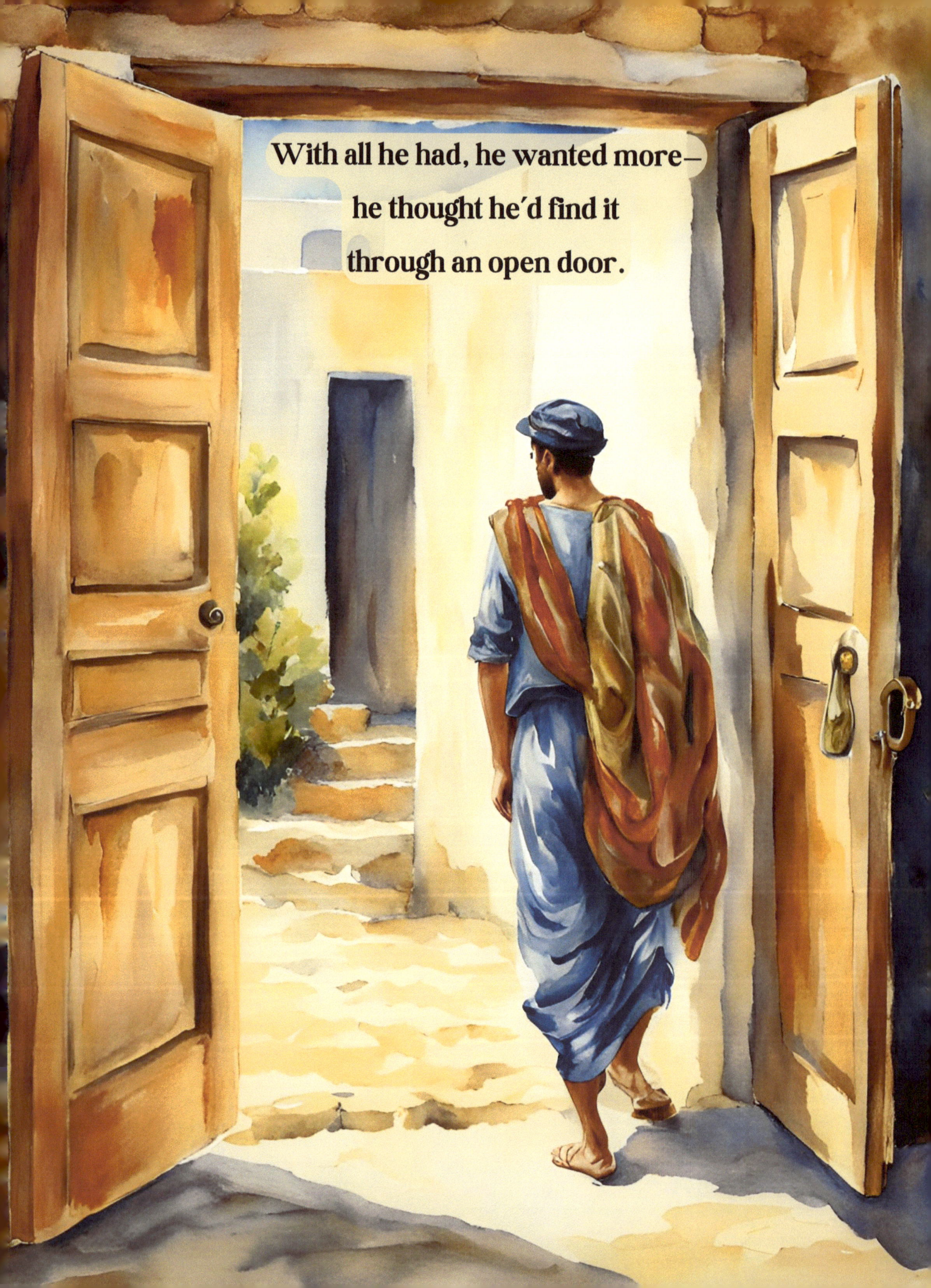

and dreams of making a brand new start.

But there's a candle in the window of his father's house that burns,

Soon his pockets were empty, and he hungered so for the way of life that he used to know.

He passed familiar fields and farms

till he fell into his father's forgiving arms,

to find a candle in the window of his father's house that burned,

the prodigal son returned.

The Prodigal Son:
Luke 15:11-24 (KJV)

11 And he said, A certain man had two sons:

12 And the younger of them said to his father, Father, give me the portion of goods that falleth to me. And he divided unto them his living.

13 And not many days after the younger son gathered all together, and took his journey into a far country, and there wasted his substance with riotous living.

14 And when he had spent all, there arose a mighty famine in that land; and he began to be in want.

15 And he went and joined himself to a citizen of that country; and he sent him into his fields to feed swine.

16 And he would fain have filled his belly with the husks that the swine did eat: and no man gave unto him.

17 And when he came to himself, he said, How many hired servants of my father's have bread enough and to spare, and I perish with hunger!

18 I will arise and go to my father, and will say unto him, Father, I have sinned against heaven, and before thee,

19 And am no more worthy to be called thy son: make me as one of thy hired servants.

20 And he arose, and came to his father. But when he was yet a great way off, his father saw him, and had compassion, and ran, and fell on his neck, and kissed him.

21 And the son said unto him, Father, I have sinned against heaven, and in thy sight, and am no more worthy to be called thy son.

22 But the father said to his servants, Bring forth the best robe, and put it on him; and put a ring on his hand, and shoes on his feet:

23 And bring hither the fatted calf, and kill it; and let us eat, and be merry:

24 For this my son was dead, and is alive again; he was lost, and is found. And they began to be merry.

Questions for Discussion:

Understanding the Story:
Who are the main characters in this parable?

Exploring Actions:
How did the father react when his son came back home?

Personal Reflection:
Have you ever been forgiven or welcomed back after making a mistake? What emotions did you experience?

Thinking Deeper:
Why do you think the father chose to celebrate his son's return? What does this reveal about his heart?

Applying the Lesson:
In what way do you think this story models how we should treat others? How can you apply this in your own life?

Reflecting on the Prodigal Son's journey, take a moment to write your own prayer. Let your words express gratitude, seek forgiveness, or ask for guidance, inspired by the love and grace shown in this parable.

_____

_____

_____

_____

_____

_____

_____

_____

_____

_____

The Illustrated Lyrics of Faith Series

The Illustrated Lyrics of Faith series features picture books for the family inspired by the Christian songs of Joe Guadagno, rooted in Scripture.

<u>Other titles in this series will include:</u>

Jonah

What Are You Waiting For?

One Touch

Climb That Mountain

Father Knows Best

Eyes of a Miracle

www.ingramcontent.com/pod-product-compliance
Lightning Source LLC
Chambersburg PA
CBHW060807090426
42736CB00002B/192